ALTERNATOR
BOOKS™

WHO INVENTED THE
LIGHT BULB?

EDISON VS. SWAN

Susan E. Hamen

Lerner Publications ◆ Minneapolis

Dedicated to my children,
who light up my whole world

Lerner Publications Company
A division of Lerner Publishing Group, Inc.
241 First Avenue North
Minneapolis, MN 55401 USA

For reading levels and more information, look up this title at
www.lernerbooks.com.

Main body text set in Aptifer Slab Regular 11.5/18.
Typeface provided by Linotype AG.

Library of Congress Cataloging-in-Publication Data

Names: Hamen, Susan E., author.
Title: Who invented the light bulb? : Edison vs. Swan / Susan E. Hamen.
Description: Minneapolis : Lerner Publications, [2018] | Series: STEM smackdown |
    Includes bibliographical references and index.
Identifiers: LCCN 2017014145 (print) | LCCN 2017024183 (ebook) | ISBN 9781512483246
    (eb pdf) | ISBN 9781512483215 (lb : alk. paper)
Subjects: LCSH: Light bulbs—History—Juvenile literature. | Electric lamps—
    History—Juvenile literature. | Swan, Joseph Wilson, 1828–1914—Juvenile
    literature. | Edison, Thomas A. (Thomas Alva), 1847–1931—Juvenile literature. |
    Patent assignments—Juvenile literature. | Inventions—Juvenile literature.
Classification: LCC TK4310 (ebook) | LCC TK4310 .H36 2018 (print) |
    DDC 621.32/60922—dc23

LC record available at https://lccn.loc.gov/2017014145

Manufactured in the United States of America
1-43334-33154-6/13/2017

CONTENTS

INTRODUCTION
A BRIGHT IDEA

f*lick!* With the flip of a switch, light fills the room as the light bulb in a lamp begins to glow a soft yellow hue. A scientist enters and sits at a desk. Colorful images illuminate the screens on her tablet and smartphone.

The scientist gets to work. Her goal is to create bulbs that will help people sleep better at night and stay alert during the day. The new technology not only illuminates a room but also affects how people respond to the light.

Modern scientists experiment with the colors of lighting to affect people's moods, among other research.

Los Angeles recently replaced all its old streetlights (*left*) with new light-emitting diode (LED) bulbs (*right*). This change will likely save about $7 million each year on electric bills.

These details are new, but the scientist's work has roots in a familiar product. The invention of the **incandescent** light bulb in the late nineteenth century changed the way people lived. Lighting a room became as simple as flipping a switch. The light that bulbs provided was much brighter than candles or gas lamps. Incandescent bulbs were steady, dependable, and far safer than an open flame. They allowed for more flexible working hours, and new businesses were launched.

After the discovery of electricity, it took inventors about a hundred years to produce light with an incandescent light bulb. But who gets the credit for the invention? Many people believe it was American inventor Thomas Edison, who tried thousands of different materials and finally found success. But what if the invention of the light bulb wasn't quite so simple? Those who have heard of British chemist Joseph Swan, who worked on some of the earliest electric lights, know there's more to the story.

CHAPTER 1
THE DEFENDING CHAMP

In 1877 Edison became interested in using an incandescent bulb to provide light for cities. At the time, gas lamps illuminated streets and homes. But gas lighting could be dangerous. The gas sometimes caused fires, explosions, or even suffocation in poorly ventilated rooms.

Edison was not the first or only player in the battle of the bulb. Many other contenders had tried and failed to design an electric light bulb that would burn long enough to rival gas lighting.

One of the first entrants into the arena of incandescent bulbs was British scientist Sir Humphry Davy. In 1802 he passed an electric current through a platinum wire. The heat from the electricity caused the wire to glow. But the light didn't last long.

Seven years after Davy made his platinum wire light, he built the first electric lamp for miners.

Inventor Warren De La Rue's main scientific interests were astronomy and photography.

In 1840 another British hopeful, Warren De La Rue, created his own light bulb design. It included a coiled thread of platinum called a **filament** inside a **vacuum tube**. Electricity passed through the filament. De La Rue's bulb lasted longer than others, but because platinum was too expensive to use for light bulbs, he was out of the game.

REVIEWING THE COMPETITION

Edison believed he could find a way to make the incandescent light bulb safe, affordable, and efficient. He learned all he could about his competition: the light bulb designs of earlier players. One of Edison's advantages came in 1879, when he improved the **dynamo**. This machine could create an electric current.

HE DID WHAT?

Edison and his assistants tested just about every filament material they could think of. Edison's lab supplies for Menlo Park included everything from oatmeal, cornmeal, and peas to human hair, peacock tail feathers (*left*), and walrus tusks. He said he wanted to have five years' worth of experiment materials on hand.

This twentieth-century drawing of Edison shows how determined he was to get his light bulb to work.

Before this, batteries had powered light bulbs. They were a very expensive power source, and many scientists dropped out of the race. But the new dynamo gave Edison a leg up— an affordable power supply that could charge a light bulb. He had the power, but could he create the bulb?

Edison knew that if he could find just the right filament, his light bulb would be successful *and* affordable. He was determined to succeed where others had failed. He planned to illuminate the world! But what would the perfect material be? Would he get to the finish line before the other scientists around the world who were also racing to create a usable bulb?

CHAPTER 2

THE CHALLENGER

As Edison struggled to find the perfect filament, another competitor was getting into the game. Would Joseph Swan, a physicist and chemist in Britain, beat Edison? He seemed to be a solid contender.

Just like Edison, Swan studied the light bulbs of earlier inventors. Swan thought De La Rue had a smart design. But he too wondered how to make the expensive platinum filament more affordable.

Swan spent ten years testing ideas before he finally developed a working bulb. He placed **carbonized** paper filaments in an empty glass bulb, added electricity, and touchdown!

Edison didn't know it, but across the Atlantic Ocean, Joseph Swan was warming up by tinkering with filament materials.

Swan's electrical workshop was a bustling place where Swan and colleagues tried to gain a competitive edge in developing new technology.

The bulb burned brightly! But this version of the bulb had two problems. First, the filament didn't last long enough. Second, there was too much air inside Swan's glass bulb. That caused the burning filament to coat the inside of the bulb with a dark layer of soot. It would be difficult to illuminate a town with sooty light bulbs. Swan was certain that removing all air from the bulb would fix this. To do so, though, he would need a vacuum pump. This device removes gas molecules from a sealed container. Swan went back to the training field.

Swan stands with technological equipment of his day in this early twentieth-century photo.

SIZING UP HIS RIVAL

With each success, a new problem arose. Swan heard rumors that the world-famous Edison was working on a usable light bulb. The pressure was on!

In 1880 Swan wrote a letter to Edison to say he was mortified to learn Edison was further along in the light bulb race. But, Swan wrote, "Now I think I have shot ahead of you." Swan's excitement grew as he tried a variety of filaments. He tinkered with possible solutions to the excess air in the glass bulb. Swan knew that to claim the title, he would need to solve that problem. But how?

The glowing wire in this picture is a tungsten filament—an important part of incandescent light bulbs.

CHAPTER 3
THE BATTLE OF THE BULB

It was 1878, the height of the battle for light bulb fame. In Menlo Park, Edison's assistants helped him test materials for possible filaments. He was certain they would eventually find one that was both durable and inexpensive. Edison believed each miss brought him closer to winning.

In this painting, Edison's team tracks how long a new bulb filament will burn.

These are some of the actual light bulbs Edison experimented with in his quest to build a better bulb.

Across the Atlantic Ocean, Swan wondered how he could improve upon his carbonized paper filament design. It wasn't enough to invent a light bulb that burned. It had to burn cleanly for long periods of time if people were going to buy and use it. Could he find something before his rival beat him to it?

Edison's team tested more than six thousand different materials. He tried cotton, linen thread, and wooden splinters. Nothing burned long enough. Finally, they tested carbonized bamboo. It produced light. Could they get it to burn for several hours?

HE DID WHAT?

This cartoon of Edison as a wizard appeared in a New York newspaper in 1879.

In **1877,** at his Menlo Park lab, Edison produced the first voice recording in history on his newly invented phonograph machine. A newspaper reporter nicknamed him the Wizard of Menlo Park, and word of his invention spread worldwide. Edison put his fame to work. He began calling himself the inventor of the light bulb, and newspapers reported this as fact. Soon many people believed the Wizard of Menlo Park had single-handedly invented a new marvel.

A VACUUM PUMP

While Edison was testing materials, Swan edged past his competition. New vacuum pumps had recently become available. With one of them, he could extract more air from his bulb. His bulb burned brightly for thirteen and a half hours without producing any dark soot. Was this it? Would Swan be the champion? He applied for and received a British **patent** and then a US patent for his bulb in 1878.

An illustration of a man at Edison's lab using a vacuum pump to take air from a light bulb

This photo offers a peek inside Edison's chemical laboratory in Menlo Park, New Jersey. This is the galvanizing room, complete with early electric light bulbs.

Not so fast! Edison wasn't out of the race yet. In 1879 a good-quality vacuum pump helped his team create an oxygen-free bulb. This bulb produced forty hours of light, almost triple the burning time of Swan's bulb!

Edison's bulb took another leap forward when he changed the shape of the filament. By curving it into a horseshoe shape, he made a bulb that glowed for one hundred hours. After further tweaks, an incandescent light bulb lasted a staggering fifteen hundred hours!

ASSIST

Lewis Latimer (*right*) was one of Edison's assistants. This young inventor designed and patented the carbon filament that helped produce Edison's long-lasting incandescent bulb. Latimer also worked at a patent law firm, where he taught himself mechanical drawing. He later drew the **schematics** used in the patent for the first telephone.

This drawing features four different kinds of light bulbs from 1882.

Edison wasted no time showing off his invention. He opened his laboratory in Menlo Park to the public on New Year's Eve in 1879. Hundreds of people stood outside, waiting to see the brightly lit electric lamps of the laboratory. Months before, however, Swan had begun installing light bulbs in some homes in England. His own house was the first in the world to have working electric lights.

In 1879 Underhill, Swan's home in England, became the first house with electric lighting.

GAME POINT

On January 27, 1880, Edison received a US patent for his incandescent light bulb. The Edison Electric Light Company began to manufacture and sell his light bulbs.

When Swan heard about Edison's patent, he sued Edison for patent **infringement**, or taking credit for Swan's work. Edison then sued Swan in 1882, claiming Swan was infringing upon Edison's patent. Edison wanted to make and sell light bulbs in Britain, but he would need to prove he was the true inventor of the light bulb. Which inventor would claim victory?

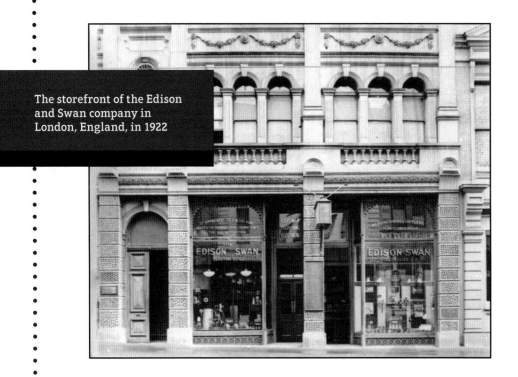

The storefront of the Edison and Swan company in London, England, in 1922

Edison's lawyers thought he would probably lose a court case. In the interest of keeping his name in the game, Edison teamed with Swan to create the Edison and Swan United Electric Light Company in Britain. The two men, once bitter rivals, were suddenly in the light bulb business together! The new company produced light bulbs and vacuum tubes.

After a tense wait, the British courts decided Edison had not invented the bulb. He had simply improved upon Swan's design. The US Patent Office agreed. Swan had won the battle of the patents—and the battle of the bulb.

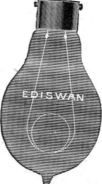

USERS

OF THE

ELECTRIC LIGHT

SHOULD SEE THAT THEIR

ELECTRIC LAMPS

BEAR THE WORLD-RENOWNED TRADE MARK

EDISWAN

EFFICIENCY

ECONOMY

The BEST and CHEAPEST in

SOLD BY THE PRINCIPAL CONTRACTORS, STORES, &C.

Head Office, Ediswan Buildings, Queen Street, E.C.

CHAPTER 4

AFTER THE BATTLE

Although Edison had lost the race to invent the light bulb, he did become the first person to successfully light a city using a power grid. On September 4, 1882, Edison opened the first commercial electric lighting and power station. It used Edison and Swan light bulbs.

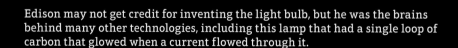

Edison may not get credit for inventing the light bulb, but he was the brains behind many other technologies, including this lamp that had a single loop of carbon that glowed when a current flowed through it.

Pearl Street Station was able to provide electricity for 1 square mile (2.6 sq. km) of Lower Manhattan, New York. That was huge for its time!

Pearl Street Station in New York City transmitted electricity to surrounding homes and businesses through an underground **conduit**. Edison had designed the system himself. His power grid and incandescent light bulbs provided affordable, effective, and long-lasting light to many homes and buildings across New York and then to other towns and cities.

These days light bulbs are so commonplace—found in everything from desk lamps and ovens to streetlights and decorative light strands—that it's hard to imagine life without them.

Joseph Swan continued to work on inventions in England. He worked with cellulose, the main substance in plant cell walls, to create a successful and widely used light bulb filament.

So who took home the gold? Edison's determination and desire for fame drove him to do whatever it took to claim glory. He never held a legal patent for the light bulb, but partnering with Swan to make the first marketable bulbs and moving on to light up New York City made him a household name. Maybe that's why so many Americans consider him the inventor of the bulb. And both inventors certainly made great contributions to this useful device. But Swan got there first, winning both the patent and the title.

THE WINNER!

SWAN

INVENTOR MATCHUP

EDISON

- **POSITION:** Businessman and inventor
- **GOAL:** Fame and fortune
- **TEAM OR SOLO:** Team
- **TOTAL PATENTS FILED (LIFETIME):** 1,093

VS.

SWAN

- **POSITION:** Chemist and physicist
- **GOAL:** Learning by inventing
- **TEAM OR SOLO:** Solo
- **TOTAL PATENTS FILED (LIFETIME):** 70

TIMELINE

1802
Sir Humphry Davy first demonstrates incandescent light using batteries and charcoal rods.

1878
Joseph Swan applies for and receives a patent for his incandescent light bulb design in the United Kingdom.

OCTOBER 1879
Edison and his team produce a light bulb with a carbonized filament that lasts thirteen and a half hours.

JANUARY 27, 1880
Thomas Edison is granted a US patent for his incandescent light bulb.

SEPTEMBER 4, 1882
Edison opens the first commercial electric lighting and power station on Pearl Street in New York City.

OCTOBER 26, 1883
Edison and Swan join forces to create the Edison and Swan United Electric Light Company.

1883
The US Patent Office declares Edison's patent for the incandescent light bulb invalid.

SOURCE NOTE

12 Joseph Swan, in a letter to Thomas Edison, September 24, 1880, quoted in Brian Bowers, *Lengthening the Day*. (New York: Oxford University Press, 1998), available online at http://americanhistory.si.edu/lighting/bios/swan.htm.

GLOSSARY

carbonized: changed into the element carbon, usually by burning or charring

conduit: a wire or tube that contains electric wires or cables and transmits electricity

dynamo: a machine that generates electricity

filament: a thin, threadlike object through which electricity can pass

incandescent: glowing with light and heat

infringement: failure to uphold the law, usually by violating someone's rights

patent: a legal document that gives an inventor the sole right to make or sell an invention

schematics: drawings that show how something works

vacuum tube: a glass tube that controls the flow of electric current

FURTHER INFORMATION

Biography: Thomas Edison
http://www.ducksters.com/biography/thomas_edison.php

de Vinck, Marc. *Electricity for Young Makers: Fun and Easy Do-It-Yourself Projects.* San Francisco: Maker Media, 2017.

Kenney, Karen Latchana. *Who Invented the Movie Camera? Edison vs. Friese-Greene.* Minneapolis: Lerner Publications, 2018.

Krieg, Katherine. *Thomas Edison: World-Changing Inventor.* Minneapolis: Core Library, 2015.

Lighting a Revolution
http://americanhistory.si.edu/lighting/bios/swan.htm

Roland, James. *How LEDs Work.* Minneapolis: Lerner Publications, 2017.

The Trailer for the Film *Edison*
http://www.pbs.org/wgbh/americanexperience/features/edison/

INDEX

PHOTO ACKNOWLEDGMENTS

The images in this book are used with the permission of: Denis Davydov/Shutterstock.com, p. 1; Oliver Wilde/Shutterstock.com, p. 4 (light bulb); iStock.com/shironosov, p. 4 (scientist); Los Angeles Bureau of Street Lighting, p. 5 (before and after); Classic Image/Alamy Stock Photo, p. 6; Wellcome Library, London, p. 7; iStock.com/AlexeyVis, p. 8; RTRO/Alamy Stock Photo, p. 9; World History Archive/Alamy Stock Photo, p. 10; Science Source, p. 11; Wikimedia Commons (public domain), p. 12; fauxware/Shutterstock.com, p. 13; Chris Hunter/Corbis Historical/Getty Images, p. 14; Daderot/Wikimedia Commons (CC0 1.0), p. 15; New York Daily Graphic. 9 July 1879/Wikimedia Commons (public domain), p. 16; Photo Researchers/Science History Images/Alamy Stock Photo, p. 17 (vacuum pump); iStock.com/photka, p. 17 (bamboo); Bettmann/Getty Images, p. 18; Granger, NYC, p. 19; Marzolino/Shutterstock.com, p. 20; C. Baldwin/Wikimedia Commons (CC by 3.0), p. 21; State Library of Queensland/Wikimedia Commons (public domain), p. 22; Print Collector/Hulton Archive/Getty Images, p. 23; Science & Society Picture Library/Getty Images, pp. 24, 27 (Swan headshot), 28 (Swan headshot); Everett Historical/Shutterstock.com, p. 25; iStock.com/ronstik, p. 26; Louis Bachrach, restored by Michel Vuijlsteke/Wikimedia Commons (public domain), p. 28 (Edison headshot); iStock.com/lushik, p. 28 (boxing glove bullets). Design elements: iStock.com/ivanastar; iStock.com/Allevinatis; iStock.com/subtropica.

Front cover: iStock.com/ivanastar (background); iStock.com/Allevinatis (boxer); Louis Bachrach, restored by Michel Vuijlsteke/Wikimedia Commons (public domain) (Thomas Edison); Denis Davydov/Shutterstock.com (light bulb); Science & Society Picture Library/Getty Images (Joseph Swan).